Oskar
RIEDING

(1840 – 1918)

Concerto for Violin and Orchestra, Op. 35
B minor / si mineur / h-moll

Edited by
Herbert Scherz

DOWANI International

Preface

The German violinist Oskar Rieding is known today for his easy violin concertos for beginners. The most famous of these is the concerto for violin and orchestra, Op. 35, in B minor, which belongs in the repertoire of every learner of the violin. It can be played entirely in the first position, although more advanced learners may play some of its passages in the third position. Our volume presents this concerto in a revised new edition with piano reduction and a new solo part with fingering marks. It enables you to learn the piece systematically at three different tempi with a professional accompaniment.

The CD opens with the concert version of each movement (violin and orchestra). After tuning your instrument (Track 1), the musical work can begin. First, you will hear the piano accompaniment at slow and medium tempo for practice purposes. At slow tempo you can also hear the violin played softly in the background as a guide. Having mastered these levels, you can now play with orchestra at the original tempo. Each movement has been sensibly divided into subsections for practice purposes. You can select the subsection you want using the track numbers indicated in the solo part. All of the versions were recorded live.

The names of the musicians are listed on the last page of this volume; further information can be found in the Internet at www.dowani.com.

The fingering marks in our volume were provided by Professor Herbert Scherz, a renowned violin teacher who for many years was professor of violin and violin methodology at the conservatories in Lucerne and Zurich. Today, after his retirement, he continues to teach very successfully on a private basis. His pupils have won more than 150 prizes at violin and chamber music competitions; many of them now have successful international careers. In 1985 he founded the "Lucerne Ministrings", an ensemble of children and teenagers up to the age of 16 that has given many concerts in Switzerland and abroad.

We wish you lots of fun playing from our *DOWANI 3 Tempi Play Along* editions and hope that your musicality and diligence will enable you to play the concert version as soon as possible. Our goal is to provide the essential conditions you need for effective practicing through motivation, enjoyment and fun.

Your DOWANI Team

Avant-propos

Le violoniste allemand Oskar Rieding est jusqu'à aujourd'hui connu grâce à ses concertos pour violon faciles pour débutants. Le concerto pour violon et orchestre op. 35 en si mineur est l'œuvre la plus connue d'Oskar Rieding et elle fait partie du répertoire standard de tous les élèves de violon. Ce concerto peut être joué entièrement dans la première position ; des élèves plus avancés peuvent cependant jouer quelques passages dans la troisième position. La présente édition a été révisée, comprenant réduction pour piano et une nouvelle partie soliste avec doigtés. Notre édition vous offre la possibilité de travailler l'œuvre d'une manière systématique dans trois différents tempos avec un accompagnement professionnel.

Le CD vous permettra d'entendre d'abord la version de concert de chaque mouvement (violon avec orchestre). Après avoir accordé votre instrument (plage n° 1), vous pourrez commencer le travail musical. Pour travailler le morceau au tempo lent et au tempo moyen, vous entendrez l'accompagnement de piano. Au tempo lent, le violon restera cependant toujours audible très doucement à l'arrière-plan. Vous pourrez ensuite jouer le tempo original avec accompagnement d'orchestre. Chaque mouvement a été judicieusement divisé en sections pour faciliter le travail. Vous pouvez sélectionner ces sections à l'aide des numéros de plages indiqués dans la partie du soliste. Toutes les versions ont été enregistrées en direct. Vous trouverez les noms des artistes qui ont participé aux enregistrements sur la dernière page de cette édition ; pour obtenir plus de renseignements, veuillez consulter notre site Internet : www.dowani.com.

Les doigtés dans cette édition ont été élaborés par Herbert Scherz, violoniste et pédagogue de grande renommée. Il fut pendant de nombreuses années professeur de violon et de la méthodique de violon aux Conservatoires Supérieures de Musique à Lucerne et Zurich et donne depuis sa retraite des cours privés avec grand succès. Ses élèves ont reçus plus de 150 prix aux concours de violon et de musique de chambre et beaucoup d'entre eux ont fait une carrière internationale. En 1985, il

fonda les "Ministrings Luzern", un ensemble d'enfants et de jeunes jusqu'à 16 ans qui se produit au cours de nombreux concerts en Suisse et à l'étranger.

Nous vous souhaitons beaucoup de plaisir à faire de la musique avec la collection *DOWANI 3 Tempi Play Along* et nous espérons que votre musicalité et votre assiduité vous amèneront rapidement à la version de concert. Notre but est de vous offrir les bases nécessaires pour un travail efficace par la motivation et le plaisir.

Les Éditions DOWANI

Vorwort

Der deutsche Geiger Oskar Rieding ist bis heute bekannt für seine leichten Violinkonzerte für Anfänger. Das bekannteste davon ist das Konzert für Violine und Orchester op. 35 in h-moll, welches zum Repertoire eines jeden Geigenschülers gehört. Das Konzert kann ausschließlich in der 1. Lage gespielt werden; fortgeschrittenere Schüler können jedoch einige Passagen auch in der 3. Lage spielen. Es handelt sich um eine revidierte Neuausgabe mit Klavierauszug und einer neuen Solostimme mit Fingersätzen. Unsere Ausgabe ermöglicht es Ihnen, das Werk systematisch und in drei verschiedenen Tempi mit professioneller Begleitung zu erarbeiten.

Auf der CD können Sie zuerst die Konzertversion (Violine mit Orchester) eines jeden Satzes anhören. Nach dem Stimmen Ihres Instrumentes (Track 1) kann die musikalische Arbeit beginnen. Zum Üben folgt nun im langsamen und mittleren Tempo die Klavierbegleitung, wobei im langsamen Tempo die Violine als Orientierung leise im Hintergrund zu hören ist. Anschließend können Sie sich im Originaltempo vom Orchester begleiten lassen. Jeder Satz wurde in sinnvolle Übe-Abschnitte unterteilt. Diese können Sie mit Hilfe der in der Solostimme angegebenen Track-Nummern auswählen. Alle eingespielten Versionen wurden

live aufgenommen. Die Namen der Künstler finden Sie auf der letzten Seite dieser Ausgabe; ausführlichere Informationen können Sie im Internet unter www.dowani.com nachlesen.

Die Fingersätze in dieser Ausgabe stammen von dem renommierten Violinpädagogen Herbert Scherz. Er war viele Jahre als Professor für Violine und Violinmethodik an den Musikhochschulen in Luzern und Zürich tätig und unterrichtet seit seiner Pensionierung auch heute noch sehr erfolgreich als Privatlehrer. Seine Schüler haben über 150 Preise bei Violin- und Kammermusikwettbewerben erhalten und viele von ihnen sind inzwischen auf internationaler Ebene sehr erfolgreich. 1985 gründete er die „Ministrings Luzern", ein Ensemble mit Kindern und Jugendlichen bis 16 Jahren, das zahlreiche Konzerte im In- und Ausland gibt.

Wir wünschen Ihnen viel Spaß beim Musizieren mit unseren *DOWANI 3 Tempi Play Along*-Ausgaben und hoffen, dass Ihre Musikalität und Ihr Fleiß Sie möglichst bald bis zur Konzertversion führen werden. Unser Ziel ist es, Ihnen durch Motivation, Freude und Spaß die notwendigen Voraussetzungen für effektives Üben zu schaffen.

Ihr DOWANI Team

Concerto

for Violin and Orchestra, Op. 35

B minor / si mineur / h-moll

O. Rieding (1840 – 1918)

DOW 4517

Oskar
RIEDING

(1840 – 1918)

Concerto for Violin and Orchestra, Op. 35
B minor / si mineur / h-moll

Violin / Violon / Violine

DOWANI International

Concerto

for Violin and Orchestra, Op. 35
B minor / si mineur / h-moll

O. Rieding (1840 – 1918)
Edited by H. Scherz

DOW 4517

II ③

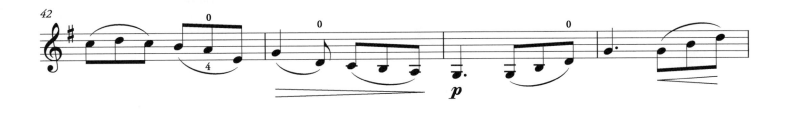

6

DOWANI CD:

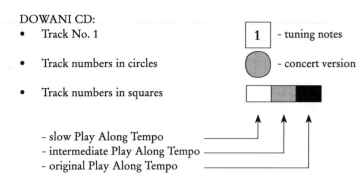

- Track No. 1   **1** - tuning notes
- Track numbers in circles ⬤ - concert version
- Track numbers in squares ▭

 - slow Play Along Tempo
 - intermediate Play Along Tempo
 - original Play Along Tempo

- Additional tracks for longer movements or pieces
- **Concert version:** violin and orchestra
- **Slow tempo:** piano accompaniment with violin in the background
- **Intermediate tempo:** piano accompaniment only
- **Original tempo:** orchestra only

Please note that the recorded version of the piano accompaniment may differ slightly from the sheet music. This is due to the spontaneous character of live music making and the artistic freedom of the musicians. The original sheet music for the solo part is, of course, not affected.

DOWANI CD :

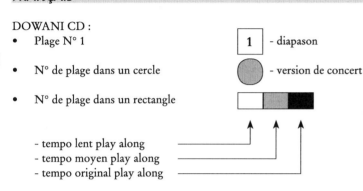

- Plage N° 1   **1** - diapason
- N° de plage dans un cercle ⬤ - version de concert
- N° de plage dans un rectangle ▭

 - tempo lent play along
 - tempo moyen play along
 - tempo original play along

- Plages supplémentaires pour mouvements ou morceaux longs
- **Version de concert :** violon et orchestre
- **Tempo lent :** accompagnement de piano avec violon en fond sonore
- **Tempo moyen :** seulement l'accompagnement de piano
- **Tempo original :** seulement l'accompagnement d'orchestre

L'enregistrement de l'accompagnement de piano peut présenter quelques différences mineures par rapport au texte de la partition. Ceci est du à la liberté artistique des musiciens et résulte d'un jeu spontané et vivant, mais n'affecte, bien entendu, d'aucune manière la partie soliste.

DOWANI CD:

- Track Nr. 1   **1** - Stimmtöne
- Trackangabe im Kreis ⬤ - Konzertversion
- Trackangabe im Rechteck ▭

 - langsames Play Along Tempo
 - mittleres Play Along Tempo
 - originales Play Along Tempo

- Zusätzliche Tracks bei längeren Sätzen oder Stücken
- **Konzertversion:** Violine und Orchester
- **Langsames Tempo:** Klavierbegleitung mit Violine im Hintergrund
- **Mittleres Tempo:** nur Klavierbegleitung
- **Originaltempo:** nur Orchester

Die Klavierbegleitung auf der CD-Aufnahme kann gegenüber dem Notentext kleine Abweichungen aufweisen. Dies geht in der Regel auf die künstlerische Freiheit der Musiker und auf spontanes, lebendiges Musizieren zurück. Die Solostimme bleibt davon selbstverständlich unangetastet.

DOWANI - 3 Tempi Play Along is published by:
DOWANI International
A division of De Haske (International) AG
Postfach 60, CH-6332 Hagendorn
Switzerland
Phone: +41-(0)41-785 82 50 / Fax +41-(0)41-785 82 58
Email: info@dowani.com
www.dowani.com

Recording & Digital Mastering: Pavel Lavrenenkov, Russia
Music Notation: Notensatz Thomas Metzinger, Germany
Design: Andreas Haselwanter, Austria

Concert Version
Alexander Trostyansky, Violin
Russian Philharmonic Orchestra Moscow
Konstantin Krimets, Conductor

3 Tempi Accompaniment
Slow:
Tatyana Gevorkova, Piano

Intermediate:
Tatyana Gevorkova, Piano

Original:
Russian Philharmonic Orchestra Moscow
Konstantin Krimets, Conductor